OPERATION SOAR 52:

Empowerment Lessons for Students

by
Dr. Sabrina Echols, M.D., M.P.H.

Copyright 2013

Published by The Noble Groups
www.NobleGroups.com
Printed in the U.S.A.
All rights reserved.

For bookings or orders
Contact Dr. Sabrina Echols
Facebook.com/sabrinaechols.3
www.DrSabrinaButterfly.org
Twitter@Sabrinaee3

Eagle Artwork by: Michael Sampson & David Elliott IV

ISBN: 978-0-9893535-8-8

OPERATION SOAR 52:

EMPOWERMENT LESSONS FOR STUDENTS

Those who hope in the Lord will renew their strength.
They will soar on wings like eagles; they will run and not
grow weary, they will walk and not be faint.

Isaiah 40:30-31 (NIV)

OPERATION SOAR 52:
EMPOWERMENT LESSONS FOR STUDENTS

TABLE OF CONTENTS

DEDICATION

To the students living in underserved and impoverished areas and those who have no voice. You have decided to SOAR and beat the odds. Be resilient and SOAR!

ACKNOWLEDGEMENTS

- My grandmother, Isabella Echols, who said, "You will complete your education or I will break your neck!"

- My teachers from St. Ambrose School (Ms. Tate), Kozminiski Academy (Ms. Boner), Curie High School (Chicago).

- Dr. Norman C. Francis, President of Xavier University of Louisiana for being the longest College President, and a great leader.

- All Professors at Xavier who pushed me: Dr. Labat, Sister Grace Mary, Sister Hurley, Dr. Butte, and Dr. Carmichael.

- Northwestern Medical School family who helped me to run the race with endurance.

- Baylor College of Medicine, Department of Family and Community Medicine for teaching Global leadership.

- Dr. Cassandra Scott, Pastor of TurningPoint Faith Church and Created2Produce Ministries for opening doors for "Operation SOAR" conference calls!

- My Pastors, Remus and Mia Wright, for opening doors for youth leaders to grow.

- Michael Sampson – Artwork for Operation SOAR 52.

- My son, David Elliott IV for graphics. My daughter, Imani, who said to "Turn Up" for the young generation.

Introduction

KILLING THE VIRUS OF MEDIOCRITY

The first day of anatomy in medical school could have traumatized and hospitalized the student with the toughest skin. I've been in love with anatomy since high school, but little did I know that this anatomy class would change my life forever. The smell of formaldehyde hit my nostrils in the hallway. I immediately became dizzy, nauseated, and delirious.

It was the best of times, and the worst of times. It was only the grace of God and "the other Grace" that sustained me. Our cadaver was without a name, but there was a tag that gave the cause of death as 'hepatic or liver failure.' I thought to myself, "Why did she die of liver failure?" So our team decided to name her "Grace." I knew only the grace of God would carry me and the team through our rigorous life-changing anatomy course. What I didn't know, was that "Grace," my cadaver, would never leave my heart.

She became a part of my sacred journey to learn to heal those with mental, physical, and spiritual ailments. Little did I know that I would always remember "Grace" and the sacrifice she made to help me learn to make people "whole." Yes, my cadaver would help me to breathe life back into those who were dead in the natural! Did she know that her decision to donate her body to science for the advancement of life would play such a powerful role in my life?

During those weak moments of wanting to throw in the towel, "Grace" would come to my heart, and I would feel guilty about my temporary emotional rollercoaster tantrums. God's grace and my other "Grace" humbled me. The deep connection with the gift of life donated by our "Grace" from God grew like seeds in fertile ground. The utmost respect was given to all cadavers! As medical students, we were never joking or taking any moment for granted. I owe my love of anatomy to "Grace." I spent a year with her and learned every muscle, nerve, tendon, bone, major organ, arteries, etc. all from "Grace."

After the cremation of the cadavers, all students attended a ceremony of prayer thanking God for the gift that was given to us. Our Anatomy professor calmly spoke words of encouragement to us and told us that throughout our journey of healing people, we would have to be committed to the process of re-learning everything we went through at least 13 times! *What? Really?*

I thought I needed to be resuscitated! Twenty years later, I can tell you that he was right! I learned that our cadavers were disguised gifts from God to keep us humble and always aware of the blessing from our Creator.

I remember when I was first granted permission to use my knife (blade) that was a part of my medical equipment and devices. I thought to myself how far I had come. From attempting to slice my enemy with a knife in grade school, to having been kicked out of Catholic School, and then on my way to becoming a juvenile, I was now saved by the grace of God. I was standing there holding the blade in my hand about to dissect out the important nerves, muscles, tissues, etc.

I'm staring at "Grace" with a knife in my hand not for evil, but for good! It was a turning point in my life. God granted me grace and mercy so I could open doors for the last, the least, and the lost. Today, I'm grateful for my blade (knife) used on "Grace," as a reminder of the pruning and cutting away process that was initiated and continues today.

Every day, I'm searching out the lost souls that need rescuing; this is what the word salvation means, 'a rescue from death.' Even when I suffer feelings of: humiliation, rejection, loneliness, unloved, undervalued, disparate treatment, racism, unequal pay, grief, betrayal, and all of the above, it's all for the glory of God! I know God loves me! Therefore, I know I am to spread this love He's extended to me, toward others. There is no turning back because of God's grace, and my "Grace."

As students of higher learning, there will be gifts given you that you know could only have come from God. You can't place a price on them. They are your divine gifts that will lift you out of a pit – gifts that will confirm your purpose and renew a right spirit in you. Embrace those gifts that only come from God. Look for no gift cards in the natural from people you meet along your pathway or material things that you desire to possess, but look for gift cards in the spirit that have no expiration date.

Our gifts and talents are promises from God that have no expiration date! You can't trade them in. They are irreplaceable. They are deeply rooted in the gospel, soul-searching truths, liberating, and full of grace!

You will also have a turning point in life that the memory of it will restore your mind to SOAR! You were born to SOAR! You are fearfully and wonderfully made (*Psalm 139:14*). You have a brain with billions of neurons, and a heartbeat that never ceases, even while sleeping. It can last an average of 3 million beats in the average lifespan. You are a walking masterpiece – you have a Circulatory System, Digestive System, Endocrine (hormones) System, Neurologic System, Immunologic System, and I can go on and on. You are authentic and are here to create knowledge! You were created to create opportunities! You were created to create greatness - not to quit on your dreams!

"Every individual has a place to fill in the world, and is important in some respect, whether he chooses to be so or not."

Nathaniel Hawthorne

You have to make the decision NOW that you will take your rightful place and fill the world. My goal is to be the voice to inspire you to take your rightful place. You are created to prosper, and reproduce, be responsible, and fill the earth... (*Genesis 1:26-27*). It's not about where you are now, but where you are going! I'm blessed that the voices from which I speak include: motherhood, prayer intercessor, physician, and entrepreneur. I've matriculated through multiple schools, from pre-K through Medical school. I am now called on daily to give advice, solve problems, implement strategies, create knowledge and opportunities. I speak into those who feel hopeless. In Scripture, hope that is deferred makes the heart sick *(Proverbs 13:12)*. Through the grace of God, I raise the oppressed and depressed –

the cast out crew, those that are isolated, and rejected by society.

I'm on the wall every day, and I refuse to come down! My passion's eliminated racial health care disparities. There are several factors involved (education, poverty, lack of health care insurance) I'm believing God that acquiring a higher education will impact racial health care disparities in our nation! I'm a watchman on the wall of education (*Isaiah 62:6*). It's just one of the ways I spread God's love. Get ready to receive and SOAR!

In this book, I will share concepts that will help you to SOAR! This book is my gift back to God and "my Grace." God is guiding my spirit to direct you to SOAR! You are created to SOAR! How can you learn to SOAR? You can soar with laser focus. Once you learn to implement laser focus, be like an eagle to teach and stir up others to SOAR! The following is a list of acronyms covered in this book to give you powerful life-long concepts that will change your life and your learning forever! These enable you to SOAR above the rest to become your very best!

Seize
Opportunities
Advance
Rewards

Listen

Avoid

Schedule

Emotional/Physical/Spiritual Health

Rise Above Rejection

Fearless Confidence

Organize

Courage

Understanding your Strength

Study/Teams

WHY SOAR?

What if I told you that 101 million children worldwide are being denied basic human rights to education? Now, what if I told you that 70 million are young girls (UNICEF). I believe if you educate a child, you can build a nation and generational curses of poverty will be broken. After visiting South Africa in March 2013, now I understand why Oprah started a school. This book is not only for students entering college and other professional schools, but it is for anyone that has made the decision to not live a mediocre life!

Mediocrity is like a virus, contagious and deadly. You have decided to SOAR! I have come to encourage your life, release your unlimited potential, and to help you seize the opportunities God has positioned you for.

The symbol we relate to SOAR is the Eagle! The USA has the American Bald Eagle as its symbol. The eagle is a mighty animal – prized and well-respected all over the world. It is a powerful bird that has a wing span of seven feet. It can glide up to 35 mph, but dive up to 99 mph.

This beautiful species doesn't know how to walk, fly, or soar when it is born. But it has the genetic coding already inside its cells to carry out every assignment! When the time is right, the parents teach the baby eagle how to fly. This process is called fledging. The mother eagle makes the baby nest extremely uncomfortable to stay. Two to three months after birth, the baby eagle begins to imitate the parent's flying around the nest. Guess what?

The eagle will never feed its children if they don't SOAR.

For the next few weeks, we will work through what it takes for students to SOAR, and we will see the difference between students who SOAR and those who do not. We will show you what happens four years later, as Student A focuses on his goals, compared to Student B who does not. Is it due to parental support, money, socio-economics, or relationships, distractions, etc? We will find out what the difference is, and how you can avoid being the next Student B. I will give you team-breathing belief strategies to learn to support yourself and your team. Throughout your journey in life, God will designate teams to guide and breathe belief in you.

Your teams will build you up and not tear you down. It will take constant belief-breathing strategies to never cease! Belief-building strategies help build your confidence, and sharpen your ability to make decisions.

This is not about me; it's about how you were created to SOAR. I'm here to empower you and to recommend that you become grateful for the journey! Don't rush the process, it is a sacred process and the joy is in the journey.

I'm presenting you with a guide which will help you expand your vision to see unlimited possibilities. You are powerless without a vision! I've come to arrest any thoughts of your giving up on your dreams! If you don't know what your purpose is here on earth, then, you are not operating in the gifts that God has given you. There are wicked plots to keep you Voiceless! You must decide now that you will not allow anyone to get you to abort your assignments! Fake friends, malicious people, gossipers, tweeters making false statements about you, and those who deny you admission to higher learning institutions, do not define your destiny. YOU define your destiny!

If you were soldiers in a war, you would receive strategies from your commander and chief officer in authority. God is that Power Source for us. He gives us strategies. Every opportunity given to you by God is a resource. Your life and all those around you will depend on whether or not you make the decision to carry out the commands given you. It's your decision! Now, disobeying commands can cause lives to be lost! So many lives are affected by your decisions. There are people that God has assigned to you, but HE is waiting on you. (Isaiah 30:18) Now, it's time to soar to give God glory!

CHAPTER 1

ZONE 52!

"Go confidently in the direction of your dreams. Live the life you have imagined."

Henry David Thoreau

When you go to a 3D movie, the person at the ticket counter will hand you special glasses to watch the movie in 3D. Now if you take the glasses off, the screen is blurry and you won't experience all that the movie intended. So pretend you are wearing 3D glasses because you are entering the Zone 52.

What is the meaning of Zone 52? This does not refer to a baseball player, or the number of a famous basketball player. It is not a construction site, nor is it the year I was born. It is not even the number of countries I want to visit. It has a far greater meaning than anything you can imagine in the world. To introduce the concept of Zone 52, let me review one of my favorite stories in the Bible.

There was a prophet by the name of Nehemiah. He had a burden on his heart to rebuild the walls of Jerusalem. The wall had been broken down for over 120 years. Now he was told about this beautiful city being in ruins and wanted to do something about it. The burden on his heart propelled him into action.

The Spirit of Nehemiah is marching deeply in my heart because when I hear the dropout rate statistics from high school and college, I cry out, "The wall is down!"

The wall is down and the gates are burned when I read about the suicide and homicide rates, especially in my hometown of Chicago, Illinois. The drug and alcohol addiction of young juvenile offenders are ridiculous. The increasing sex-trafficking cases are overwhelming! The wall is in ruin as I hear about more prisons being built, and more schools being closed.

Let's not overlook young men and women aborting their assignments. Students start off in a major they are passionate about, but change their course due to modern day conspiracy plots! Viruses and anguish of mental, emotional, physical, and spiritual poverty overwhelm us! Abrupt fearful changes are all around us!

Look around and you will see that many, many walls have been destroyed all around you. Get your boots on because you will learn how to build a wall. Don't expect to enter Zone 52 with flip flops on your feet!

After completing my freshman year at Xavier University of Louisiana, I had a flashback while entering Zone 52. I learned my mother had rented my room to our cousin. I no longer had a bed! Therefore, when visiting home during college, I would sleep on family member's couches, and sometimes their floor. This process kept me humble and in the Zone. Thoughts of "I have no bed to sleep in" kept me motivated to build my wall. It's been over 20 years, and I still quote "I have no bed to sleep in." It is the fuel to my rocket!

Recently, my son, David returned home from his first year of college at Xavier University. He reported how he noticed students lost their focus within the first two to three weeks of their freshman year. Some students made drastic changes from one major to another; this induced stomach spasms!! Why, did they lose their focus? Were they having financial problems? Did they have a belief team? Today, college tuitions are at the highest rates in our history. You can't afford to lose focus! This dilemma has me writing out plans and strategies for students to find their way out of the maze of fear into their God given purpose. It is one of the key strategies to eliminate poverty and health care disparities.

Nehemiah gives us numerous examples of how to be a courageous, faithful servant. As a cup-bearer, his job was to serve the King. The first thing Nehemiah did was pray about his fellow brethren in captivity and the Wall of Jerusalem. One of my favorite sayings is, "Pray about everything." Then, Nehemiah asked the King for the resources to go to Jerusalem to rebuild the city. The King granted him favor. The scripture never mentions Nehemiah's background as a builder, carpenter, bricklayer, painter, etc. But, Nehemiah had a burden that pushed him into action.

If someone would have told me when I was a young college student, that I would someday be writing about the burdens on my heart that have propelled me into action, I would have laughed them right out of my face. I always struggled with writing essays and with misspelled words. My struggle was so great that during high school, my aunt hired a tutor to help me with creative writing.

Nevertheless, Nehemiah went to Jerusalem and began to structure teams of families to rebuild the wall. He pressed forward unselfishly with courage, faith, and determination to see the wall complete. It took

Nehemiah only **52 days** (Nehemiah 6:15) to rebuild a wall that was broken down over 120 years! That was a miracle!

Before Nehemiah started on his journey to rebuild the wall, he prayed. He spent three days praying and fasting. This is one of the greatest weapons of warfare you will ever possess! You can defeat any enemy with prayer and fasting! I'm a witness!

You don't have to offer long prayers. Just pray God's word back to Him and it will not be returned void. He is waiting for you to validate his promises! Great rewards come when you speak God's words to Him.

"So will My word be which goes forth from My mouth; It will not return to Me empty, without accomplishing what I desire, and without succeeding in the matter for which I sent."

Isaiah 55:11

When you keep moving forward, the enemy will lose confidence. (Nehemiah 6:15)

"Therefore submit to God. Resist the devil and he will flee from you."

James 4:7

Nehemiah had three enemies around him as he gave instructions to the families that were rebuilding the wall. I am here to unveil the modern day mountains that have been built to capture you into slavery and keep you there. Let me warn you that you will have enemies to this assignment. They will come to assassinate your journey. You must commit to action and enter Zone 52!

In the book of Nehemiah, chapter two, after praying and receiving resources from the King, Nehemiah went to Jerusalem. He observed the gates which had been destroyed by fire! He told the few men that traveled with him that he had the favor of God and then he said, "Let us arise and build." (Nehemiah 2:20)

Don't be surprised when enemies begin to speak against your dreams. That is all a part of the process. I'm telling you that you will have opposition! If you think you will never face opposition in your endeavors, you are no longer breathing. Presently, I open doors for the uninsured and those living in poverty so they can receive health insurance. The opposition to keep people in poverty has been so great that I know that I must be on point. If you don't have any opposition in life, you have to question whether or not you are making a difference.

Nehemiah had three enemies: Sanballat, Tobiah, and Geshem. These enemies came to taunt, mock, and belittle him. You may face negative family members, toxic teachers, or even counselors that will laugh about your decision to move forward. They have come to assassinate your dreams and visions. It is not your responsibility to explain to negative people the reasons why you want to SOAR. They won't receive your reasons, because they are walking in foolishness and not in wisdom. Foolish behavior can lead to a death sentence. Trust me, as a medical director, I sign death certificates!

However, when the families completed their wall assignment successfully, the sarcastic enemies were nowhere to be found! Nehemiah's faithfulness had blown them away. I stand in the gap and breathe belief into the lives of those who have lost hope in their dreams and to the younger generation who have no voice. This book is for those who lack guidance, and information to build the wall. In 52 days, you will learn to implement 52 new affirmations, and 10 action items to help you SOAR like an Eagle!

You were not created to walk around like a chicken, but to SOAR like an Eagle and take charge over everything on earth! It's your choice whether to enter Zone 52 or not.

You will gain wisdom and knowledge that you can act on, or you can pretend that you don't know, (deliberate ignorance), and live a mediocre or reckless life. It's your choice! Will you take the "Zone 52" challenge or not?

Over the next 10 weeks, you will be memorizing 52 scriptures. Once you memorize these scriptures, allow them to become a part of your life. These scriptures will sustain you for the rest of your life. During these weeks, we will also examine your vision, belief-breathing strategies, and laser focus techniques. These are wisdom and instruction tools that will help you develop clarity for what you see ahead for your life. That is your vision. You will develop and write out your vision if you don't already have one. Get ready for 10 weeks of being challenged and pushed to SOAR.

S = **Seize**

O = **Opportunities**

A = **Advance**

R = **Rewards**

This is my Vision:

_____

_____

_____

SCRIPTURES TO SOAR ON

DAY 1   "Write the Vision and make it plain on tablets, that he may run who reads it." (*Habakkuk 2:2*)(NKJV)

DAY 2   "Commit your way to the Lord; trust in Him, and He will do this." (*Psalm 37:5*)

DAY 3   "My people are destroyed from the lack of knowledge." (*Hosea 4:6*)

DAY 4   "Where there is no vision, the people are unrestrained, but happy is he who keeps the law." (*Proverbs 29:18*) (NASB)

DAY 5   "For I know the plans I have for you," declares the Lord, "plans to prosper you and not to harm you, plans to give you hope and a future." (*Jeremiah 29:11*)

CHAPTER 2

VIRTUAL REALITY

"Have you not known? Have you not heard? The everlasting God, the LORD, The Creator of the ends of the earth, neither faints nor is He weary. His understanding is unsearchable. He gives power to the weak, and to those who have no might He increases strength."

Isaiah 40: 28-29

Eagles' eyes are extremely powerful, having up to 3.6 times human acuity for the martial eagle, which enables them to spot potential prey from a very long distance *(Source: Wikipedia.org)*. Without the Eagle's vision, they could not see their prey, and they would perish.

"Even the youth shall faint and be weary, and the young men shall utterly fall, but those who wait on the LORD shall renew their strength. Those who hope in the Lord will renew their strength. They will soar on wings like eagles; they will run and not grow weary, they will walk and not be faint."

Isaiah 40:31

You have memorized the first five scriptures and now they are in your heart. Did you take time out of your busy schedule to write your vision? If you can take time to check your cell phone, social sites, and text messages, then you can time take to write your vision. It's that important because when you know your vision, that is what will help motivate you and keep you moving forward.

"For the vision is yet for the appointed time. It hastens toward the goal and it will not fail. Though it tarries, wait for it; for it will certainly come; it will not delay."

Habakkuk 2:3

I'm here to help you expand your vision to see unlimited possibilities. As *you "write the vision and make it plain,"* embrace your ability to create more opportunities. Then you will see the clarity of your purpose. You are powerless without a vision! It's as if you are born, and are blind without purpose. You can decide to stay blind or you can decide to create knowledge that will lead you into the light!

Connect to a mentor to stir up the gifts inside of you. Don't stop looking until you find the right mentor - someone who recognizes the gifts in you and will not let you abort your dreams! I have an entire team of mentors!

"There are nearly 150 million poor and near poor people in America who are not responsible for the damage done by the Great Recession. Yet they pay the price. The poor did not create the de-industrialization of America, unmatched corporate profiteering and greed, more than a decade of foreign wars, and unregulated tax benefits for the wealthy... Nearly one third of the American middle class--mostly families with children have fallen into poverty." *(The Rich and the Rest of US by Tavis Smiley and Dr. Corneal West)* I'm a witness to this nuclear attack on the poor and working families of America.

God gave me a heart to open health care centers for the underserved. I collaborated with health care centers to open their doors to the uninsured. An employee from my malpractice insurance company discouraged me and wanted me to abort my assignment. He mentioned that their company was changing its policy and I could no longer be protected as a Medical Director collaborating with mid-levels. So, I had to get coverage with another company. I did not take it personally, because I'm aware of the schemes to keep the underserved population in a poverty mindset. It was a fear strategy aimed against me to get me off the wall. *(Nehemiah 6:3)*

Poverty is a disease! The arrow, of discontinued malpractice insurance coverage shot at me, did not hit a target! I began to send up nuclear bombs, which were spiritual warfare prayers to destroy the demonic plans that were trying to provoke me to abort my dreams. Now, I'm repeating that same strategy to protect you as students and aspiring leaders from losing your dreams. I am aware of the fear and scare tactics the enemy uses to try to paralyze your actions and my actions.

I've come to write into your hearts, "It's not where you are that matters; it's where you are going." Your assassinators want you to stay ignorant, unhealthy, and in poverty. But the enemy is a liar! You may appear to be in a "Voiceless" state, in poverty, overridden in silence, hopelessness, or defeat. But I come to speak into your dry bones! *(Ezekiel 37)* Come Alive!

You are in charge of the Action Plan of your life!

Life and Death are in the Power of **your** tongue! *(Proverbs 18:21)*Action increases your confidence in the area of your passion. Your faith, trust and belief in God will activate your faith and your dreams! That's right! You were born to live out and fulfill your God given dreams! I believe if you continue to speak a thing until you see it manifested, it will drive your behavior to make it manifest. Action will expose your weaknesses, and your self-imposed limitations! Ponder these questions:

- Do you want it? You define "it."
- How badly do you want it?
- Are you willing to sacrifice for it?
- Do you know who you are and your purpose in it?
- Do you know how to sustain it?
- Why do you want to go to college? Why do you want to graduate?
- What do you want your experience to be?
- Who do you want to work with?
- What type of lifestyle do you want to live?
- Why do you want a family? When are you going to get started on YOU!

Now, be specific in what you want and need. When a blind beggar, named Bartimaeus, called to Jesus for help, Jesus said, "What do you want Me to do for you?" The blind man replied, "Rabboni, that I may receive my sight!" Jesus said, "Go your way; your faith has made you well." *(Mark 10:51-52)* Learn to be more specific about where you want to work, what type of career you want, and the person you want to marry. Then, write out how likely you are to carry out those specific requests. Where is your commitment level on a scale of 1 to 10?

"Do you want to be made whole?" Jesus asked the man who was crippled for 38 years. *(John 5:6)* Are you ready to go through the actions needed to reach your dreams? Are you ready to persevere even if people don't believe in you? Are you ready?

Zone 52 will keep you on the right track!

What is your PASSION?

What is it that you are PASSIONATE about?

_____

_____

_____

SCRIPTURES TO SOAR ON

DAY 6   "Take delight in the Lord, and He will give you the desires of your heart." *(Psalm 37:4)*

DAY 7   "Stand firm, hold your position, and see the salvation of the LORD on your behalf,..." *(2 Chronicles 20:17)*

DAY 8   "God is my fortress where I will never be shaken." *(Psalm 62:2)*

DAY 9   "Do not merely listen to the word, and so deceive yourselves. Do what it says." *(James 1:22)*

DAY 10   "Teach me to do Your will, for You are my God; may Your good Spirit lead me on level ground." *(Psalm 143:10)*

CHAPTER 3

MISSION POSSIBLE

"It always seems impossible until it's done."

Nelson Mandela

In 7th grade, I was barely passing science. I had no passion for the study of life. Science projects were a gruesome task for me. However, in 10th grade, I experienced a 360 degree turnaround. My biology teacher at Curie High School *(Chicago, IL)* started to breathe belief in me. She felt I would do great in science.

My plans were to live in New York, dance, and be in Broadway shows. God had a different plan and sent my teacher to speak into my life. Great things happen when you breathe belief. It won't cost you anything, but it can elevate the least likely person to succeed.

Self-love is extremely important in building belief! You never stop working on you. Self-love is not ignoring others, or being selfish. It is taking time to build your confidence and self-esteem so that you can be a Servant Leader and pour into others when the time is right in your life. You are not selfish when you are practicing self-love; you are learning to build yourself up so that you can serve others. Others may not understand the Zone 52 life in which you are living. This is not the season in your life to make other people understand your goals and dreams. When you are in Zone 52, this is the time to trust God's plan for your life and not man's plan.

My Nehemiah journey, which eventually led me to my Zone 52, started at age 14, when I decided to become a Servant Leader for God. I chose the medical profession and went into intense preparation. Twelve years later, at the age of 26, I received my medical degree from Northwestern University in Chicago. It was just the beginning of my journey. Learning about public health, receiving a Master's degree, and three years residency training were all part of my preparation. I continued to grow, learn, and absorb. Every career move prepared me for what I do now. I just continued to press forward, *(Philippians 3:13,)* no matter what was going on in my life.

The challenges were great, but they were my best learning experiences for growth. My problems became my blessings. When you read my bio, you won't read how I had a tutor for English in high school to help with the ACT and SAT pre-college exams. You won't read how I had to take and retake my: senior competency essay college exam, my biochemistry and physiology exams in medical school, my U.S. medical license exam, or my board certification! It was all a part of my Nehemiah journey. I made a decision not to come off the wall.

**The mission was possible all along when
I believed it was possible.**

Have you ever read or entered a study where the researcher said you can take the real medicine or a placebo (no medicine). Now the placebo pill looks just like the pill that contains the real medicine. In fact, the pills look identical. However, the placebo gives a false appearance that it is the real thing. It tricks the mind.

Many studies report that the group on placebo starts to have positive results even though they lack the real medicine because they think they have the real pill. The placebo pill inspires a person to change behavior without really giving them medicine. The pill is empty. There are multiple studies that show the placebo confuses the mind. It's fake, but the thought of real medicine can trigger positive results!

This leads me to raise the question about your belief system. For example, two male students enter the same college as freshmen, have the same race, background, socioeconomic status, and same major. We follow them both until graduation. Four years later, one graduates on time and enters professional school. The other student struggles for the next two years and finally graduates, but settles for any job, and will reconsider graduate school.

Why did the student A do so well, compared to Student B? Was it due to parents, money, distractions, social networking, etc? The difference is one has a team breathing belief and one lacks an adequate team. Success takes constant belief breathing strategies that never cease! Believe breathing strategies help build confidence, and sharpen ones decisions.

You are the message! Do you look like you believe in yourself? Do your actions now support your beliefs? If you were on an admission or interview committee, would you fight for you?

When you go on an interview for college, graduate school, or a job, and they ask if you have any flaws, how do you respond? Who wants to speak of their weaknesses? The Bible says in II Corinthians 12:9, "My strength is made perfect in weakness." Therefore, God will give you grace to strengthen and grow you out of your flaws! We have to embrace God's strength! He can bear all things. Give God your burdens. He can turn any bad circumstance around.

Read about all the people in the Bible whom God used despite their flaws. Joseph was in prison. Moses doubted he could lead the Hebrews out of bondage because of speech problems and his past sins. Rahab was a prostitute. Gideon was the weakest of his tribe. Esther was an orphan. Ruth was a widow and followed her mother-in-law into a foreign country.

Job was sick and lost everything he owned including his children! Jeremiah felt he was too young. Nehemiah was a cup-bearer to a king and did not have equipment or experience to build a wall. Apostle Paul, former prosecutor of Christians, was shipwrecked. David was a shepherd boy who was forgotten by his father when the prophet Samuel came to anoint the next King. Later after becoming king, David committed adultery and had the woman's husband killed. But all of these people were used mightily by God and the Word of God still speaks of them today being relevant to us. We are benefiting today from the work that God did in and through them.

Now see, you are in great company! They all had flaws, of course. Almighty God used each one of them to make a profound difference in the lives of those around them. You can too; you can make it! Just Believe!

SOAR BELIEF:

I Believe

_____

_____

_____

SCRIPTURES TO SOAR ON

DAY 11   "I can do all things through Christ Who strengthens me." (*Philippians 4:13*)

DAY 12   "If you can believe," said Jesus. "Everything is possible for one who believes." (*Mark 9:23*)

DAY 13   "Therefore I tell you, whatever you ask for in prayer, believe that you have received it, and it will be yours." (*Mark 11:24*)

DAY 14   "Do not be anxious about anything, but in every situation, by prayer and petition, with thanksgiving, present your requests to God." (*Philippians 4:6*)

DAY 15   "I am the Lord, the God of all mankind. Is anything too hard for Me?" (*Jeremiah 32:27*)

CHAPTER 4

LASER FOCUS

"Education is the ability to listen to almost anything without losing your tempter or your self-confidence."

Robert Frost

LASER

L = Listen Before You Leap Into Action

A = Avoid Distractions And Traps

S = Schedule

E = Emotional/Physical/Spiritual Health

R = Rise Above Rejection

L = Listen Before You Leap into Action

In the operating room, before surgery takes place, there is a team of people carrying out different duties, but one goal. Unity is pleasant to the Lord, and will save lives! (*Psalm 133:1*).

The surgical nurse must listen to the anesthesiologist to know when the patient is asleep and ready for the anti-septic soap to scrub the particular body part exposed for surgery. The surgeon has to wait until the nurse completes the cleansing process on the patient. The surgeon listens to the anesthesiologist before the first incision is made on the body. The nursing teams listen to the surgeon in order to hand off the correct instruments needed and help to keep order and a smooth flow in the operating room. Listening to every team player will yield a successful surgery! The skill of listening keeps people alive!

Nehemiah also established order in Jerusalem after the wall was built. "Now the wall was rebuilt and I had set up the doors, and the gatekeepers and the singers and the Levites were appointed..." (*Nehemiah 7:5*)(NASB)

It is critical to develop great listening skills to help you advance to the next level. I spend 80 percent of my daily routine listening! I earnestly listen to ideas, problems, trials, medical concerns, etc. However, learning to make critical decisions always starts off in silence. Silent prayer and mediation are key factors in developing great listening skills. Listening to your inner voice and thoughts can influence your life. After listening, you repeat back the most important information you received. This requires that you take the time to explain conflict. Know that your priorities for solving problems may not be exactly the way the person you are listening to would handle a task.

Learn how to rank priorities. Get back to what's important in pursuing your passion! Analyze your current situation, job, or educational process. Is the current school or job the right fit? Don't make rush decisions based on your emotions and your current circumstances. Remember you cannot define yourself by your circumstances.

Always seek wisdom and understanding. (*Proverbs 4:5*) Wisdom will help you make better decisions with the knowledge received. Your goal is to maintain balance in your spiritual, physical, and emotional life. If you get out of balance start Zone 52 over, and activate your Laser Focus.

A = Avoid Distractions and Traps

Distractions and traps such as social media, sex, alcohol, drugs, credit cards, negative people, texting while driving, drinking while driving, etc. are high-risks behavior and put your vision in jeopardy. If you received a letter in the mail offering you a $1,000 Gift card, of course you would be excited. Just the thought of selecting new updated electronics such as an iPad, iPhone, iPod touch, or an Apple TV would certainly get your attention. The instructions in the letter, however, go on to require a meeting at 3 a.m. in the parking lot of a deserted area. Are you still excited? Finally the date of the meeting to pick up the card is the same day you have to take a test or are scheduled for a job interview. Will you be tempted to go? Will you interrupt what you are doing and go?

Can't you just imagine people camping out in lawn chairs, with tents and coolers and the line stretching for 10 miles, waiting for that free gift card!!

Taking time off from your routine schedule to focus on that gift card will not add value to your life. It will not get you closer to your goal. Keep your eyes on the One who gives the rewards, not on the actual physical or material rewards. (*Hebrews 2:2*)

The great thief of the night doesn't always come in the night! The thief comes to steal and can come in at anytime, especially via the airwaves! Learn to turn phones and social media off when focusing on a goal. Watching fake reality shows may be entertaining, but will not get you closer to your goals.

When my son went on a student ambassador program in China, he reported that social media is banned in China. The world is looking for China to be one of the most powerful nations in the next few years. Successful leaders do not spend enormous amounts of time on social media. They pay people to keep up their websites and maintain their media accounts. They have marketing or public relations teams in place to help them with their image and keep up with the latest trends. Some successful leaders hire their teenagers!

I explain to students, you will never receive a master's degree in Twitter, or a doctorate in Facebook. What other people are doing and saying and eating is none of your goal-oriented, mind-set business.

You are scheduled to submit an essay by 9 a.m., on a specific day. While preparing your assignment, you decide to take a break and check in on your social media site that has false stories, gossip, and people posting pictures of their meals! This is not a good use of your time. The entire world is tracking your life and routine while you post from your Smart phone and your iPhone onto social media. Do we really have privacy or confidentiality when reporting anything?

No matter how long my day has been or how exhausted I may feel at the end of the day, I never go to sleep without reading a medical article, or leadership book, and Bible. My phone is on silent. I have learned to protect my quiet time. Waking up early everyday, even on the weekend, helps me to not rush through my time of meditation and praying. I can't start my day without spending quiet time reflecting on our Maker, our God of love.

If you chase a career, a man or a woman, materials things such as, designer clothes, purses, shoes, jewelry, cars, houses, for the gain of money--you will be disappointed! It's called self-sabotage or self-retaliation and it is hazardous to your health and goals. Once you enter college, working two or three jobs while trying to complete your graduation requirement will most likely slow down and postpone your target date! You have the rest of your life to work jobs, and mature in your character.

I'm aware that working part time may be necessary to meet financial burdens while pursing your dreams and goals; however, this is about keeping your priorities in order. With the rising costs of education, in the most expensive institutions it is not cost effective to stretch out or extend your studies. Just, "Get It Done."

After college, I had a huge credit card debt. I read, Suze Orman's book, "The 9 Steps to Financial Freedom," and it helped me to budget and to get my financial life in order. Let go of your wants and focus on your present needs! When I go shopping now, I ask myself, "Do I want or need this item?" If I need it, "Do I need it today or can it wait until next month?"

For a short period of time in your life, you will need to discipline yourself and avoid purchasing designer bags, shoes, clothes, etc., especially if you cannot afford them. Resist charging items and running up your credit card balances. If you don't have cash to purchase necessary items, beware of falling in the valley of debt! You cannot afford to live your life burdened with credit card debt. It is not a part of your divine inheritance. It blocks your ability to possess the land. You are created to possess the land! (*Joshua 18:3*).

S = Schedule/Set Up Priorities

Discipline is the key ingredient to set you up to SOAR! Place everything on a schedule. Everything from spending time at church, time with family, study time, work time, fun time, it all goes on a schedule.

Learning to say, "No," to meetings, parties, and other events will help keep you focused. You will not be able to go to every Fourth of July barbeque or wedding, or graduation, or concert. I promise when you complete your goals, you will have so much more time to attend family and fun events. You are in the midst of intense preparation for life and most people who have not been in your shoes will never be able to relate to you.

Here is a tip on saying, "No." Rehearse this statement to diplomatically decline an invitation. "Thank you for the invite, however, I'm so sorry that I am unable to make your event due to a conflict in my schedule. However, please keep me in mind for your next event." This is a polite, "NO!" Your event may be studying in the library or meeting with your mentor for a one on one coaching session. Your event is in keeping with your goal to succeed.

I was always envious of my professors who took off on Fridays! While training as a resident, we worked twelve to fourteen hour days, including Fridays while our attending doctors and professors were off playing golf. You probably can't get an appointment with your cardiologist or doctor on a Friday if they love golf!

So now, guess what? I do not schedule any patients on Friday's. Friday is my day for me! That is my day for pampering, reading, relaxing, whatever I want to do. Friday is special time with my family, acting goofy with my kids, dancing in my living room or pretending we are at the club. We have a family joke, "Let's go to the club!" Then, we drive home and dance in our living room. We know how to throw a party!

When I was in college, medical school and residency while studying and in preparation to meet my dreams and goals, I had to decline multiple invitations that would have deterred me from those goals. But now, as promised, I have the opportunity to set my schedule as I desire. I had to say, "No," during those educational years, but now I get to say, "Yes," to whatever pleases me and my family.

Pull the plug on procrastination now in your life! Yes, procrastinating will assassinate your goals. Waiting to study the week of the final is much too late. Yes, you can cram, but your body will pay a steep price. However, if you designate study time on a routine basis, you won't panic at the end of your semester.

E = Emotional /Physical /Mental/ Spiritual Health

Learning to control your emotions will liberate you!

You cannot control other people's actions, so you should not become attached to a positive or negative outcome! You are in control of how you react to circumstances, but God is in control of the outcome. Therefore, learn to control your emotions so that you will remain full of energy and power! Studies show that a student's immune system before they enter college as compared to their immune system during finals at the end of one school year will show a drastic decrease! Why? This is due to many stress factors relating to school. Factors such as: financial problems, relationship issues, work, trying to mingle with organizations, joining a fraternity or sorority, and pressure to excel in school or get into graduate school.

Instead of being reactive, be proactive. Everyday speak positive words to get your attitude in check. Create a personal mission statement that inspires you to get up and move! Read your daily scripture in the mornings before leaving home. Keep in close contact with your mentor because when you face adversity, you won't faint!

If you are experiencing depression, anxiety, loneliness, anger, or any emotion; ask your mentor to help you with facing the issue and pressing your way through! You will have an attitude of gratitude if you decide to work on your emotions!

R = Rise Above Rejection

When Nehemiah's enemies heard that he was rebuilding the Wall, they became angry, and used abusive language to intimidate him and the workers. "What are these feeble Jews doing? Are they going to restore it for themselves? Can they offer sacrifices? Can they finish it in a day? Can they revive the stones from the rubble even the burned ones?" (*Nehemiah 4:2*)

No need to verbally address all the arrows directed to you that will fly by day and night. The conspiracy of getting you to come down off the wall will come in the form of money; drugs; alcohol; sexual encounters; fake friends; psychotic bosses; counselors who discourage you from pursuing your goals; or loved ones who will laugh at you. But I believe that you will pass the test because you won't come off the wall! Nehemiah did not change his clothes for 52 days! (*Nehemiah 4:15-17*) He remained focused and on task.

The family teams that were helping to build the wall had tools in one hand and their weapons in the other hand. (*Nehemiah 4:11*) Your weapon is the word of God. It will demolish everything that comes to destroy you. Ask for strength. (*Nehemiah 6:8-9*) Memorize each of the assigned scriptures during your 10 weeks and you will see that no weapon formed against you will be able to prosper. (*Isaiah 54:17*)

Nehemiah prayed and went into the best action plan, he just kept building anyway!! Your pressing forward will increase your confidence and cause you to accomplish your goals.

I was amazed when I read how many times Abraham Lincoln lost elections before becoming the

16th President of the United States. His rejection was his elevation. He started off sweeping the floors of the law office and library before pursuing his passion to become a lawyer. He was not born a president. He had people teaching, coaching, and breathing belief into him all the way to the White house.

Mary McLeod Bethune inspires me to build because she was born to parents who were once slaves. As a child, she learned to read and write and stayed on the wall. Mrs. Bethune started a college, which became, "Bethune-Cookman University," in 1904 in Daytona Beach, Florida. (Source: Wikipedia).

Sojourner Truth went to battle for freedom for her son and the case went all the way to the US Supreme Court, and she won. She didn't know how to read or write, but she stayed on the wall. While staying on the wall, you will get dirty, you will be hungry, you will become fearful, anxious, lonely and more, but don't come down off the wall!

Learning to walk away from ungodly influences will be a key tool as you detect foolish characters in your presence. "The fear of Lord is the beginning of knowledge; Fools despise wisdom and instruction." (Proverbs 1:7) (NASB) You will save yourself time, money, and progress; and your mental health will remain healthy when you know that fools hate knowledge and will die for a lack of understanding. (Proverbs 1:22, 10:2)(NASB)

Spend time reading the faith chapter, Hebrews 11. Read and absorb the entire chapter. The lessons and stories contained in that chapter will become a catalyst for your faith.

FOCUS

F = Fearless Confidence

O = Organize

C = Courage

U = Understanding your Strength

S = Study/Teams

Do you have a hard time focusing and eliminating distractions? Do you get distracted by loud noises, flashing lights, people talking around you, or do you take breaks every 5-10 minutes. Are you interrupting yourself, checking your phone, your social media, downloading pictures, and checking the latest fashion trends on the internet? Distraction and attention span activity involves certain areas of the brain *(the prefrontal cortex and the parietal cortex)*. You can be strong in one area, for example, your focus *(prefrontal cortex)*, but weak in the other area which controls your distractions *(parietal cortex.* Therefore, it is extremely important to work on both your focus and your distractions, because these are controlled by different areas of the brain.

An article from a 2007 edition of USA Today, stated, "This ability to willfully focus your attention is physically separate in the brain from distracting things grabbing your attention," said Earl Miller, a neuroscientist at the Massachusetts Institute of Technology. He led the study, published in the Journal of Science. Where are you focusing your efforts? What and who are your biggest distractions? I notice that my son can study with music playing but my daughter has to have complete silence. Television, CD's, radio and any other audio must be turned off while she is studying. She wants complete silence! They have completely different studying and learning styles.

You have to train your subconscious mind what is important for you to focus on and that toxic trash must be eliminated immediately. You have to be committed for the rest of your life to training your brain about what is an important distraction and what is garbage. If you enter an Emergency room for treatment with a sore throat and fever and another person enters with chest pain and shortness of breath, my brain is going to tell me to triage the patient with the chest pain first. Chest pain and shortness of breath can present as life threatening medical conditions. We are trained to respond to life threatening medical problems and to know the difference between life threatening and non-life threatening diseases. I believe that you will learn to daily prioritize what is important in your life and not allow worldly distractions to influence you or detour you away from your goals.

F = FEARLESS CONFIDENCE

Overcoming Fear Of Failure: The Great "Body Snatcher"

It's time that you become Faith Focused and not Fear Focused. Think about how Nehemiah focused his prayers to ask God for guidance pertaining to rebuilding the wall in Jerusalem. He served the King, and this position put him in favor with the King. He asked the King's permission to go rebuild his ancestor's city, and he was given timber from the King's forest and letters of safe passage for travel. God turned his fear into favor because he believed in the calling on his life. I believe you will receive supernatural courage and favor to face the mountains that will come along your journey! In my daily routine as a mother, prayer intercessor, doctor, business owner, etc., I share my testimony, in my first book, "Voiceless." I share the love of God with those who are struggling with who they are and with those making horrible decisions based on fears. Living in fear and anxiety is at an all-time high. Fear of failure, fear of illness, fear of poverty, fear of nuclear war, fear of fear itself, and fear of focus are all death sentences. Fear will destroy your dreams, and snatch you out of greatness! I've come to kill all your fears that block you from growing and pursuing your passion. Learn to chase your fears.

I can recall the day I cut away at the fear of swimming. I waited to take swimming classes until I was a senior in college! I felt so silly in that swimming class learning how to hold my breath under water, while the other students were swimming laps. I learned to chase my fears! If you fear speaking in public, practice; record or videotape your voice. Chase your fears and never back down because your faith is being tested. You can, and will pass the test!

Defeating fear will become a natural act in your life. Defeat feelings of inferiority, low self-esteem, and low ambition. Focus on what you will receive by walking it out. Chase your fears by seeking the knowledge and experience you need to grow in confidence. Then go into action. Action destroys fear!

Practice over, and over, and over and your fear will shrink away. Open your mouth daily and declare the truth about who you are and defeat any fears that are holding you hostage.

O = ORGANIZE

When I hired a professional organizer to help me organize my closets and filing system in my home office, it was as if I was paying for pain. She made me sit with her and organize three piles: Keep, Trash, and Recycle. I had to sit and throw out all the things I felt were important, but in reality, they were actually obsolete. We created more bags of trash than bags of recyclables during that session. Out with the trash! That was painful. The pile of items that I would "keep," filled the smallest bag, but clearly they were the most important valuables.

Among the items in the "keep" pile were pictures of my children growing up and awards they had received! Priceless! The filing system cleared the clutter so that I could operate in an effective and efficient manner. If you don't throw out trash it becomes toxic, sending off a foul odor which can become harmful to your body. When you unplug yourself from toxic people that are polluting your thoughts, you can build any wall anywhere you step! Get your life completely in order, which includes your body, your mind, and your spirit! You will dream bigger and hit every target according to God's will.

Ask yourself these questions concerning everyone and every situation; "Are these people helping me or hindering me? Will attending this event help me or hinder me?" Spending time arguing with people who don't understand your goals is a hindrance. Is someone or something holding you back from completing your goals? Are you your own stumbling block because you don't believe you are ready for the next level?

C=COURAGE

I will instruct you and teach you in the way you should go; I will counsel you with my loving eye on you.

"Be strong and courageous. Do not be afraid; do not be discouraged, for the Lord your God will be with you wherever you go."

Joshua 1:9

You have a made up mind that you are moving forward no matter what circumstances you face. The family teams that Nehemiah put in place to build the wall were discouraged after coming out of Babylonian captivity with no resources. They were in debit, and many had lost their land. Nehemiah not only built the wall in 52 days, but he demanded that all property be returned and all debt be canceled! (*Nehemiah 5:11-12*) That is courage.

"Watch, stand fast in the faith, be brave, be strong." (*1 Corinthians 16:9-13*)

"Execute by seeing, believing, and you will receive!" (Mark 11:24).

U=Understanding your Strength

You don't have to be a copycat or yearn for someone else's gift. Search out and learn to recognize the gifts that God has given you. Perfect your God-given gifts. When you understand your strength, you won't worry about who likes you or who approves of your goals and dreams. You will pull the plug on spending time with people who have no goals and surround yourself with those who seize opportunities and stretch your thinking.

You may not think or feel that it is so while you are in the midst of it, but one day you will be grateful for all the trials and obstacles you will learn to overcome. You won't blame others for your mistakes, but you will stand firm and be accountable. Turn your mistakes into miracles. You will come into alignment with what God's will is for your life. "Whether therefore ye eat, or drink, or whatsoever ye do, do all to the glory of God." (1Corinthians 10:31)

S = Study/Team

Your journey in life will involve teams that have been assigned to you to keep you moving on your path! John C. Maxwell wrote, 'The Law of Teamwork." He said teamwork will help to accelerate your goals. This is what Nehemiah carried out. He enlisted teams of families to help rebuild the wall. He also set up watchman on the wall to defend against the opposing teams coming to destroy their work. You will also have opposing teams.

Nehemiah and the other builders were united in their efforts and took shifts guarding their rebuilding efforts. They never stopped working until the goal was completed. Fifty-two days later, the wall was completed!

Your schedule will reflect what's important to you. You need to write your schedule on paper or place reminders in your phone or iPad. Make your schedule visible. Also, consider mounting a dry eraser board in your room with weekly or monthly spaces. Highlight the most important activities of your week. You will not be able to make all the activities that you would like to, therefore, learning to prioritize events will help you eliminate activities contrary to your goals.

Procrastination is a disease that will set up a crooked root in your life and demolish your dreams. Procrastination is not your friend! It robs you of your hope. You must decide to pull the plug on procrastination and defeat its disguised tactics when they begin to arise.

In this chapter, I have shared some laser focus strategies to help you stay on course. Now, I want you to stop and let us pray together so that our Heavenly Father can come and bind together your goals and commitments with His purpose for your life, and by faith, you will be covered, equipped, and empowered for the journey ahead. Not only that, by faith, I believe you will also be empowered to the finish line to become a leader and light-bearer for the next generation without a voice!

Dear Heavenly Father,

I thank you for _____ who has submitted a request to successfully pass their exams and tests.

You are the Creator of Heaven and Earth. You formed us in your image (Genesis 1:26) and you told us that you knew us before we were formed in our mother's womb (Jeremiah 1:5). Father, you know the plans you have for _____. Plans to prosper him/her, to give them a future and hope. (Jeremiah 29:11). Your Word says that _____ is fearfully and wonderfully made (Psalm 139:14).

I'm asking for supernatural recall when _____ take the test/exams. You said that if we are in need of wisdom, to ask and it will be generously given to us (James 1:5). I decree and declare that memory storage of the brain will be whole, perfect, and complete. The brain area that receives words and speak (Broca's) and the area that understands/interprets what it hears (Wernicke's) will be aligned to your will. We decree and declare all hormones/emotions will be stable and there will not be any loss of nerve cells due to toxins (i.e. alcohol, drugs, nicotine). We demand that every demonic plan to destroy the memory comes to an abrupt halt.

We snatch out any fear that blocks _____ from completing their goals. We come against fear of failure, inferiority syndrome, lack of ambition, lack of persistence, low self-esteem, feelings of hopelessness.

We ask the Holy Spirit to guide _____ . Lord, you said we can do all things through you because you strengthen us (Philippians 4:13). Father, take away the worry and the unnecessary concerns. Block distractions that keep _____ from completing goals. Take away ungodly friends out of their path and reveal supernatural decision-making power.

Thank you for the Power and Authority to move by faith to complete the assignments you have given _____.

We will give you all the Glory in Jesus' name we pray! Amen.

SOAR LASER FOCUS: Things I need to cut out to become more productive and effective:

_____

_____

_____

SCRIPTURES TO SOAR ON

DAY 16   "I sought the Lord, and He answered me; and He delivered me from all my fears." (*Psalm 34:4*)

DAY 17   "The Lord is my light and my salvation whom shall I fear? The Lord is the stronghold of my life; of whom shall I be afraid." (*Psalm 27:1*)

DAY 18   "...The Lord does not look at things people look at. People look at the outward appearance, but the Lord looks at the heart." (*1st Samuel 16:7*)

DAY 19   "Keep watching and praying that you may not enter into temptation; the spirit is willing, but the flesh is weak." (*Matthew 26:41*)

DAY 20   "Keep this Book of the Law always on your lips; meditate on it day and night, so that you may be careful to do everything written in it. Then you will be prosperous and successful." (*Joshua 1:8*)

Chapter 5

"Virus"

**"He who opens a school door,
closes a prison."**

Victor Hugo

When preparing a patient for an operation, the fingers, hands and arms up to the elbow of the team members are scrubbed vigorously with a special anti-bacterial soap. Your attire consists of scrubs, surgical mask, sterile gloves, and a gown. To complete your uniform you must wear coverings for your head and shoes. You are covered from head to toe to protect you from contaminating the patient, and the field from infection. There is even a specific order of dressing yourself to remain sterile. Everyone in the entire Operating Room is scrubbed and dressed in the same manner.

During flu season, thousands of lives are lost every year because of the flu virus. If you get the flu, it could possibly have you down for the count for two to three weeks. A flu virus will be a huge distraction in your life. It could also be fatal. Many people take flu vaccines to prevent catching the flu. In like manner, avoid known distractions that may cause a contagious virus to delay your dreams or destroy your life.

Indulging in anything in excess can take you off your course. Excessive partying, club-hopping, separation anxiety from your cell phone, your iPod or your iPad, excessive eating, sleeping, shopping, etc., can all contribute to leading you astray from your goals. Not saying that you can't get back on course, but it takes longer, and time will have been wasted. Time is a gift from God.

Fake dates, friends, and social organizations can cause you to have a detour in life that will take you longer to get to your destination. Avoid people that are arrogant, haters of good, lovers of self, etc., as referenced in II Timothy 3:1-5.

Watch out for those who would mutate on you! Like a virus, they will change their ways and behaviors to trick you into a toxic lifestyle. Then, as soon as you are in their click, they will take off their mask and reveal their true substance.

Misplaced perception will disrupt your priorities. If you buy a designer purse or shoes for $300 and you know that you don't have extra money above your necessities to make such a purchase, you have just stepped into the danger zone. We all have been in the danger zone. However, you can control how long you stay in that danger zone. Once you are out of that zone, you can control if you will return.

Credit card debt takes time to pay off, especially if you are a college student without a job, or working for minimum wage. You can't afford to always satisfy your desires. For the time being, just focus on your needs and unplug yourself from a Fantasy Lifestyle, until you have completed college or graduate school and can afford more luxury items.

Don't be ashamed to shop at a thrift store or the Goodwill and consignment stores. Trust me no one will know you paid $3 for a t-shirt.

SOAR SUCCESSFUL ATTITUDE:

_____

_____

_____

SCRIPTURES TO SOAR ON

DAY 21   "God opposes the proud but shows favor to the humble." (_James 4:6_)

DAY 22   "If any of you lacks wisdom, he should ask God, Who gives generously to all without finding fault, and it will be given to him." (_James 1:5_)

DAY 23   "Everyone who is arrogant in heart is an abomination to the LORD." (_Proverbs 16:35_)(ESV)

DAY 24   "For God so loved the world that He gave His one and only Son, that whoever believes in Him shall not perish but have eternal life." (_John 3:16_)

DAY 25   "You will rejoice in all you have accomplished because the Lord your God has blessed you." (_Deuteronomy 12:7_)

CHAPTER 6

"GET IT DONE"

"If you can't fly then run, if you can't run then walk, if you can't walk then crawl, but whatever you do, you have to keep moving forward."

Dr. Martin Luther King, Jr.

You may be asking, "How do I run the race that God has for me?" You must learn how to activate your faith. Know that God is the Author and the Finisher of your faith. (*Hebrews12:1-2*) You must hear His word, speak His word, and then do it. You are not running the race for your parents, your family, or your mentors. You are running the race for yourself to give God the glory!

When you know and walk into your divine purpose, the race is preliminary. It is not authentic yet. It's like watching the Superbowl pre-game show. The actual game, "kick-off," is not until the pre-game show ends. You will decide when your walk into your divine purpose begins. You only need faith the size of a mustard seed, and nothing will be impossible for you. (*Matthew 17:20*)

"There is an appointed time for everything." (*Ecclesiastes 3:1*) There are 168 hours in a week. Be persistent when you schedule times for prayer, study, church, meals, breaks, movies, fun, dates, parties, and exercise. Don't drive yourself crazy if you do things out of order, or switch things around on your schedule. Just, "Get it done!"

You may be thinking, "It's a boring life that is on a schedule!" WRONG! You will find that those who live by a schedule get more things done and are less likely to procrastinate than those who simply function on a whim. You will have plenty of time to be spontaneous, in the future. Now is not that time. You need to, "Get it Done." With the rising cost of college, healthcare, the housing marketing, etc., you can't afford not to complete your assignments.

I know for a fact that people will pay for your knowledge! After you learn to work hard, you will be able to play hard.

SOAR PERSISTENCE:

I am Persistent in

_____

_____

_____

SCRIPTURES TO SOAR ON

DAY 26   "Whoever disregards discipline comes to poverty and shame, but whoever heeds correction is honored." (*Proverbs 13:18*)

DAY 27   "Diligent hands will rule, but laziness ends in forced labor." (*Proverbs 12:14*)

DAY 28   "No discipline seems pleasant at the time, but painful. Later on, however, it produces a harvest of righteousness and peace for those who have been trained by it." (*Hebrews 12:11*)

DAY 29   "Ask and it will be given to you; seek and you will find; knock and the door will be opened to you." (*Matthew 7:7*)

DAY 30   "Consider it pure joy, my brothers and sisters, whenever you face trials of many kinds, because you know that the testing of your faith produces perseverance." (*James 1:2-3*)

CHAPTER 7

"SEARCH ALERT"

HOW DO I SUSTAIN MY DREAM?

"Let us more and more insist on raising funds of love, of kindness, of understanding, of peace. Money will come if we seek first the Kingdom of God - the rest will be given."

Mother Teresa

Connecting with positive people will ignite a harvest of positive thinking. Its feels like training for the Olympics. London, England was the host country for the 2012 Olympic Games. Over 10,000 athletes participated in the Games from 204 National Olympic Committees. Gabby Douglas was the first African American to win an individual Gold medal in the all-around Gymnastics competition. Interestingly, before the Olympics, we did not know anything about her. Gabby started preparing for the Olympics years prior to her 2012 event.

Who is prepared to win the race? Who is willing to go above and beyond what is required? Who is mentally capable of overcoming adversity and obstacles? I'm not looking for those who are physically strong, but those who have an incredible desire to keep moving forward no matter what confronts them. I call that group, faith walkers.

No matter how long it takes, showing up at the Olympics and not trying to win the Gold is not an option! The Hebrew writer said, "Therefore, since we have so great a cloud of witnesses surrounding us, let us also lay aside every encumbrance and the sin which so easily entangles us, and let us run with endurance the race that is set before us, fixing our eyes on Jesus, the author and perfecter of faith, who for the joy set before Him endured the cross, despising the shame, and has sat down at the right hand of the throne of God." (*Hebrews 12:1-2*)(NASB)

This means you are authentic and you are not on earth to run your parent's race, or your children's race. You have to make a final decision that this race will be run by you and only you. Comparing yourself to your siblings, co-workers, or business partners is like committing suicide. You will cut off your own oxygen.

The enemy wants you to abort your dreams. Through doubt he will try to convince you that you are not tall enough; or unable to speak publically; or unable to complete your education due lack of resources; or you are too short in statue; or on and on! Pull the plug on that doubt talk! It is not supportive of your dreams and goals.

Nehemiah understood the importance of physical and spiritual walls and gates in Jerusalem. Sustaining the wall and gates will be a personal lifetime commitment. It helps you continue to grow emotionally, academically, culturally, and physically. You never stop growing! You have the willpower to exercise self-control, consistency, and persistence.

SOAR SUSTAINABILITY:

I will increase my self-control in

_____

_____

_____

SCRIPTURES TO SOAR ON

DAY 31   "But the fruit of the Spirit is love, joy, peace, patience, kindness, goodness, faithfulness, gentleness and self-control. Against such things there is no law. Those who belong to Christ Jesus have crucified the sinful nature with its passions and desires." (*Galatians 5:22-24*)

DAY 32   "...but hospitable, a lover of good, self-controlled, upright, holy, and disciplined." (*Titus 1:8*) ESV)

DAY 33   "...to slander no one, to be peaceable and considerate, and always to be gentle toward everyone." (*Titus 3:2*) (NIV)

DAY 34   "Peace I leave with you; my peace I give you. I do not give to you as the world gives. Do not let your hearts be troubled and do not be afraid." (*John 14:27*)

DAY 35   "But seek first His kingdom and His righteousness, and all these things will be given to you as well." (*Matthew 6:33*)

CHAPTER 8

WHO DO I TRUST?

DECEPTION

"The roots of education are bitter, but the fruit is sweet."

Aristotle

Young biblical leaders that trusted God and were tested over and over again inspire me to put all my trust in the Creator of everything. I love reading about young biblical leaders like Joseph, King David, King Josiah, Jeremiah, and Timothy. Also I'm so impressed with how worldly leaders yielded their lives to God and made a major impact on our lives: President Abraham Lincoln, Dr. Martin Luther King, Jr., President Nelson Mandela, and Mother Teresa.

Blessings will follow you when you trust God. Your parents can't show up at your college or job and carry out your duties for you. They can't do your online homework, or they would be committing fraud. It is your responsibility to be accountable for your actions. Your mentor will help you in this area and you will have supernatural growth! However, don't rely on teachers and counselors to give you all the information you need about opportunities in your field. You have to do it yourself. Lack of ambition, will create a valley of darkness. Now is a good time to rehearse the 5 W's. They are:

1. What do I want?
2. Why do I want it?
3. What's my strategy?
4. Who will be my mentor? To whom will I be accountable?
5. When am I expecting to get it?

SOAR TRUST:

Unlock the door to the Prisoner of War--Unbelief.

"Education is the key to unlock the golden door to freedom."

George Washington Carver

Unbelief is a Prisoner of War. It keeps you locked up. These are things you do to unlock that door.

1. Spending time alone in the presence of God.
2. Reading His word and praying scriptures back to God.
3. Knowing the Character of God.
4. Knowing who we are in Christ.
5. Hearing the Word, speaking the Word, then doing the Word.
6. Thank God for the answer in advance.
7. Keep a positive and right attitude.

SCRIPTURES TO SOAR ON

DAY 36   "The Lord has made me strong." (*1 Samuel 2:1*)

DAY 37   "You faithfully answer our prayers with awesome deeds, O God." (*Psalm 65:5*)

DAY 38   "Having hope will give you courage." (*Job 11:18*)

DAY 39   "Trust in the Lord with all your heart and lean not on your own understanding, in all thy ways acknowledge Him and He shall direct your path." (*Proverbs 3:5*)

DAY 40   "If you remain in Me and My words remain in you, ask whatever you wish, and it will be given you." (*John 15:7*)

CHAPTER 9

CHANGING COURSES

Leap of Faith—
How Do I Keep Balance in My Life?
Stability in Body, Mind, & Spirit

"All great achievements require time."

Maya Angelou

A GPS system in a car will navigate your driving directions from one location to another. The GPS system is a robot, providing audible directions, and instructing you to follow its commands. If you make a wrong turn, your directions will be recalibrated and you are asked if you want the new directions downloaded to the GPS system. If instructed, the system will download the new directions, turn by turn. You are not a robot! Your life is so valuable, that God is the only One that you should trust when it comes to directions for your life. You should trust only God to guide your steps.

Take some time to consider your "faith requests." Be sure they are from your heart, not from the top of your head or your EGO. You must long for your requests and believe in them. You must be willing to travail and agonize over your requests, and then search out and claim God's promises for them.

Are you praying according to the will of God? Are you praying for God's purpose and His kingdom or your own? You very well may receive a college degree. But is your degree reflective of your passion? You may obtain an accounting degree, but end up owning a flower shop because you love flowers. You must be willing to sacrifice your wants to follow your passion!

I want to be in Paris, France right now, but I need to open doors for the underserved population to help improve their lives. I want to fly to Chicago and spend the day with my grandmother shopping and eating desert, but I need to coach and teach health care providers who will have an impact on decreasing health care disparities in this country.

When you know you have a calling on your life, it's easy to sacrifice. "For the LORD God is a sun and shield; the LORD bestows favor and honor, no good thing does He withhold from those who walk uprightly." (*Psalm 84:11* (ESV) Your life will be a journey of favor!

"For he who finds me finds life And obtains favor from the LORD.

Proverbs 8:35

SOAR FAITH:

Write down your faith confessions to keep close by:

_____

_____

SCRIPTURES TO SOAR ON

DAY 41   "Now faith is confidence in what we hope for and assurance about what we do not see." (Hebrews 11:1)

DAY 42   "And without faith it is impossible to please God, because anyone who comes to Him must believe that He exists and that He rewards those who earnestly seek Him." (Hebrews 11:6)

DAY 43   "...If you have faith as small as a mustard seed, you can say to this mountain, 'Move from here to there,' and it will move. Nothing will be impossible for you." (Matthew 17:20)

DAY 44   "The eyes of the Lord watch over those who do right." (1 Peter 3:12)

DAY 45   "Give all your worries and cares to God, for He cares about you." (1Peter 5:7)

DAY 46   "If God cares so wonderfully for flowers that are here today and thrown into the fire tomorrow, He will certainly care for you..." (Luke 12:28) (NLT)

CHAPTER 10

HOW TO KEEP SOARING
Benefits & Rewards

**"The only true wisdom is in knowing you
know nothing.**

Socrates

Rewards: Knowledge is a Lifestyle

I emailed my son a notice from a research company which I received. The research company asked me to sit down for 30 minutes to answer questions about a commercial regarding cholesterol medication. I asked my son to share the notice with his friends to remind them that while they may feel that they are missing out on parties, and fun, people will pay for your knowledge.

You don't know who they are or when the opportunities will come, but I promise, people will pay you for the knowledge you will create! People are waiting to pay you for the knowledge you will acquire over your lifetime! How you apply the knowledge to empower the lives of others will be vital to soar! However, you have to commit to increasing and staying updated in your field of endeavors.

What's interesting about this particular research, is even if I make a mistake and give them a wrong answer, my voice will still be heard. Stop worrying that you may give a wrong answer. Just ask God to give you wisdom and understanding to say the right things at the right time. Your voice will be heard by somebody.

If I asked you for a tape player, or a record player to play music you would look at me strangely. No one uses record players, video cassette records, or tape players anymore. You would probably remind me that those things were used in the past. Current technology has provided DVR's, CD players, the iPod, the iPad touch and Smart phones and now music can be downloaded from the internet. Change never stops changing!

Your time is now! The past is gone the future will one day be your present and then become your past. Your next is now! Now is the time to build. Build the wall that no man or circumstance will ever destroy.

Spread your wings. Know that the rest will come after you have fallen to the ground and sustained injuries that you do not want to repeat. Most of these injuries are emotional wounds, such as depression, guilt, and hopelessness. Just like a toddler throws a tantrum because the mother will not give him candy, you sometimes will find yourself behaving or thinking that way. Eventually the toddler stops after diving to the floor multiple times and getting up with bumps and bruises on his head – so will you!

Proceeds from my first book, "Voiceless," are directed toward scholarships for underserved students and the Dr. Richard Wainerdi Wellness Center. Since then, the Lord spoke to my heart and told me keep writing to open doors for students whose parents are incarcerated, or living with cancer, HIV or AIDs.

Just like Nehemiah had a burden for the oppression of his people and their safety in their homeland, the oppression of students is the burden on my heart. Building the wall was Nehemiah's mission, and building a wall of empowerment for students like you is my mission! Nehemiah along with the teams of families and the prophet Ezra established order and transformed the people with the Word of God. That is also my goal for you to keep soaring!

I have a journal in which I record prayers that God has answered for me and other prayers that I am continuing to lift up through intercession. This journal is one of the greatest gifts I have; it reminds me of how gracious and compassionate our God is. Reading and going through this journal at times helps me to keep soaring and standing in the gap for you and your excellence. You may be working part time in a grocery store bagging groceries, but be faithful and strive for excellence! This will help you to keep soaring!

"Be faithful in small things because it is in them that your strength lies."

Mother Teresa

SOAR GRATITUDE:

I will always give thanks for

_____

_____

SCRIPTURES TO SOAR ON

DAY 47   "Whatever you do in word or deed, do all in the name of the Lord Jesus, giving thanks through Him to God the Father." *(Colossians 3:17)*

DAY 48   "Finally, brothers and sisters, whatever is true, whatever is noble, whatever is right, whatever is pure, whatever is lovely, whatever is admirable—if anything is excellent or praiseworthy—think about such things." *(Philippians 4:8)*

DAY 49   "Wise words bring benefits, and hard work brings rewards." *(Proverbs 12:14)*

DAY 50   "You will enjoy the fruit of your labor. How joyful and prosperous you will be!" *(Psalm 128:2)*

DAY 51   "You are the most excellent of men and your lips have been anointed with grace, since God has blessed you forever." (Psalm 45:2)

DAY 52   "Let us not become weary in doing good, for at the proper time we will reap a harvest if we do not give up." *(Galatians 6:9)*

Now SOAR, My Chosen Generation!

My intention for sharing these strategies with you is not to get any special recognition, or awards. My purpose is to equip you to pursue your passion and sustain it. When you take this information and pass it on, that will be the greatest gift you can give back to me and you will be glorifying God.

OPERATION SOAR 52 is a demonstration of what happens when you yield your thoughts, words, actions, and life to the Holy Spirit. I invite the Spirit to rise up in me every day so that I might walk in a spirit of excellence for the glory of God. I have stumbled many times in the past, and will most likely stumble again. However, I'm renewed by God's mercy and His loving-kindness. The Bible says in II Corinthians 12:9, "His grace is sufficient for me, and my weakness is made perfect in His strength"

Remember, you are a gift to the world, and creating knowledge is a part of your purpose! Pass on your greatness everywhere you go! This is my gift to you over 52 days! You are my Chosen Generation, and a Treasure of the Heart! Now, SOAR!

**"For where your treasure is, there your
heart will be also."**

Matthew 6:21

BIBLIOGRAPHY

Echols, Sabrina, MD, MPH. *Voiceless: Inspiring True Voice Lessons on Life*. Houston: Noble Groups, 2013. Print.

Howard, Clark, and Mark Meltzer. *Clark Smart Parents, Clark Smart Kids: Teaching Kids of Every Age the Value of Money*. New York: Hyperion, 2005. Print.

Http://en.wikipedia.org/wiki/Eagle?

Http:// en.wikipedia.org / wiki /Mary_McLeod_Bethune

Neergaard, Associated Press, Lauran. "Separate Brain Areas Rule Concentration and Distraction." *USA Today* 29 Mar. 2007: n. pag. Print.

Omartian, Stormie. *The Power of a Praying Parent*. Eugene, Or.: Harvest House, 2005. Print.

Smiley, Tavis, and Cornel West. *The Rich and the Rest of Us: A Poverty Manifesto*. New York: Smiley, 2012. Print.

ABOUT THE AUTHOR

Sabrina Echols, M.D., M.P.H.

A VOICE FOR THE VOICELESS

WWW.DRSABRINABUTTERFLY.ORG

• P.O. BOX 84721 • PEARLAND, TX 77584

Dr. Sabrina Echols was born in Chicago, IL. She attended Curie High Performing High School where God gave her a vision to become a doctor in order to promote health and enhance the lives of the medically underserved. Her mandate from the Lord is to open doors for voiceless generations – those who cannot speak for themselves. She is a Magna Cum Laude graduate of Xavier University in New Orleans, LA. Dr. Echols earned a medical degree at the prestigious Northwestern University Medical School in Chicago, IL. She became a community advocate and also earned a Masters in Public Health from the University of Illinois in Chicago, IL.

Dr. Sabrina Echols completed residency at Baylor College of Medicine (Houston, Texas) Department of Family Medicine in 2000. She completed a Fellowship in Leadership/Faculty Teaching in the Family Medicine Department. Dr. Echols joined the faculty in 2001-2007 and became Assistant Professor at Baylor College of Medicine, caring for patients, teaching medical students/residents, and performing clinical research in the area of breast cancer prevention.

Dr. Echols now contracts with major health care facilities in Houston, Texas promoting wellness, home health care, and prevention. She is currently Medical Director of Central Care Community Clinic in Houston. She is also the founder and CEO of non-profit, Butterfly Wellness. Dr. Echols breathes belief into the lives of others. She is the founder of a weekly conference call, "Take God as your Business Partner," and Operation Soar – a college student leadership mentoring program. Dr. Echols also has a scholarship program for minorities pursuing health care studies at Xavier University in Louisiana. She is a Senior Director in Mary Kay Cosmetics where she teaches leadership skills to empower families.

A servant leader in her community and abroad, Dr. Echols is a prayer intercessor at The Fountain of Praise Church (Houston, TX) and serves as a leader in The Wellness Ministry there. She is also a prayer intercessor on international Prayer Ministry Calls with Dr. Cassandra Scott of Created2Produce in Houston, Texas. Honored as one of Houston's Top 25 Women in 2011, and receiving a Certificate of Congressional Recognition from Congresswoman Sheila Jackson Lee for Central Care Community Health Center in 2012, Dr. Echols is well-known for empowering communities in community health and wellness, and has been a platform speaker at many women's empowerment & health events. She travelled with the Metamorphosis team, The Fountain of Praise Church to Brazil and South Africa to minister at the Metamorphosis International Conference. She is also a member of Delta Sigma Theta Sorority, Inc. Dr. Sabrina Echols is the blessed mother of son, David and daughter, Imani, and resides in Pearland, Texas.

CONTACTS:

Facebook.com/sabrinaechols.3
www.DrSabrinaButterfly.org
Twitter@Sabrinaee3

www.ingramcontent.com/pod-product-compliance
Lightning Source LLC
LaVergne TN
LVHW051154080426
835508LV00021B/2618